fun origami for child...

Dino!

12 daring dinosaurs to fold

Mari Ono & Hiroaki Takai

CICO **Kidz**

Published in 2017 by CICO Books
An imprint of Ryland Peters & Small Ltd
20–21 Jockey's Fields, London WC1R 4BW
341 E 116th St, New York, NY 10029

www.rylandpeters.com

10 9 8 7 6 5 4 3 2 1

Text © Mari Ono and Hiroaki Takai 2017
Design and photography © CICO Books 2017

A CIP catalog record for this book is available from
the Library of Congress and the British Library.

ISBN: 978 1 78249 466 9

Printed in China

Designer: Alison Fenton
Photographer: Geoff Dann

In-house editor: Dawn Bates
Art director: Sally Powell
Head of production: Patricia Harrington
Publishing manager: Penny Craig
Publisher: Cindy Richards

Contents

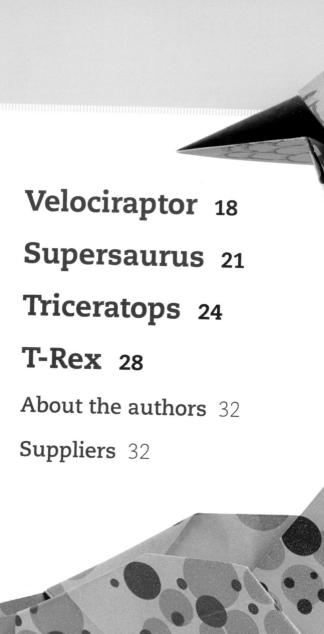

Welcome to Origami!

Here is a collection of 12 fun paper dinosaurs for you to make, either by yourself or with a grown-up if you prefer. Begin with a simple project and learn a few basic folds before moving on to something a bit more ambitious. You'll soon find yourself picking up the skills that Japanese people have been using for centuries and making models that even origami masters would be proud of. Origami is great fun and we hope you will enjoy bringing the models to life.

Key to arrows

Fold
Fold the part of the paper shown in this direction.

Folding direction
Fold the entire paper over in this direction.

Open out
Open out and refold the paper over in the direction shown.

Change the position
Spin the paper 90° in the direction of the arrows.

Change the position
Spin the paper through 180°.

Turn over
Turn the paper over.

Make a crease
Fold the paper over in the direction of the arrow, then open it out again.

Look for the dinosaur!

A good project to start with

Move on to level 2

Perfect your skills with level 3

Basic Techniques

Origami is a very simple craft that simply requires a steady hand and some patience. Before you start making your first model, just check over these simple tips to ensure every paper model you make is a success.

Making folds Making the paper fold as crisply and evenly as possible is the key to making models that will stand up as the designs intend—it really is as simple as that.

1 When you make a fold ensure that the paper lies exactly where you want it, with the corners sitting exactly on top of each other.

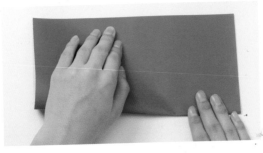

2 As you make the crease, be sure to keep the paper completely still so that the fold is straight.

3 Still holding the paper with your spare hand, use a ruler or perhaps the side of a pencil to press down the fold until it is as flat as possible.

Opening folds

Sometimes you will need to open out a crease and refold the paper so that it lies in a new shape, as in the triangle fold shown here.

1 Lift the flap to be opened out and begin pulling the two sides apart.

2 As the space widens you will need to be sure that the far point folds correctly, so use a pencil to gently prise the paper open.

3 As the two corners separate, the top point drops forward and the two edges open out to become one.

4 Press down the new creases to make the two new angled sides of the triangle.

Reversing folds

To reverse a crease you will need to open out your model and gently turn part of the paper back on itself. This can be tricky so practice on a spare piece of paper first.

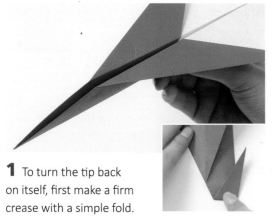  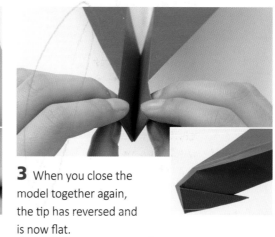

1 To turn the tip back on itself, first make a firm crease with a simple fold.

2 Return the tip back to its original position and open out the model. Turn back the nose again along the fold you just made.

3 When you close the model together again, the tip has reversed and is now flat.

When you're using scissors, ask a grown-up to supervise or help.

Scutosaurus (scut-o-sore-us)

Scutosaurus, meaning "shield lizard," had bony plates of armor just beneath its skin, including its cheekbones, which were very large. Although it had a tough exterior, Scutosaurus was a slow dinosaur and an easy target for predators.

1 Place the sheet of 10in (25cm) square paper with the design face down. Fold the corners into the center, then turn over and fold the corners in again.

2 Turn the paper over and fold forward the top edge of the paper along the center line.

3 Lift the right-hand side, then press the point forward, refolding the flap into a triangle. Turn over and repeat.

4 Lift up the paper and let the model open out slightly.

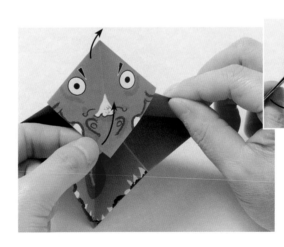

5 Press back the head from the point at the top, making a crease across its widest part and letting the lower flap come out. Fold forward the remaining two flaps to form the base for the head.

Chomp! Scutosaurus couldn't chew—it swallowed stones to grind food in its stomach!

Anchiceratops (an-ki-seh-ra-tops)

Anchiceratops, meaning "horned face," lived in North America around 72 million years ago. Its skull included a big shield that protected the upper part of its head, as well as a pair of tough horns. When you have made your model, have fun opening and closing his mouth. Having a big mouth was very handy for Anchiceratops because it was a very greedy dinosaur!

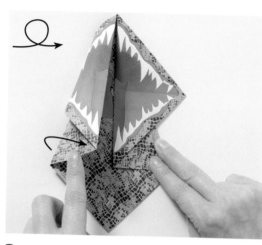

1 Place the sheet of 10in (25cm) square paper with the design face down. Fold the paper from corner to corner to make a crease, and open. Repeat for the other corners. Now fold the corners to meet at the center. Fold the corners in once more.

2 Turn the paper over and fold in the outer points so that the edges run down the middle of the model. Lift the model and allow the loose flaps to lie flat on top.

3 Turn over the top of the model, making the fold line across the widest part of the piece, and let the top flap out from behind the model.

4 Turn the model over and fold up the loose flap, then slightly open the side flaps at the back to allow the dinosaur to stand up.

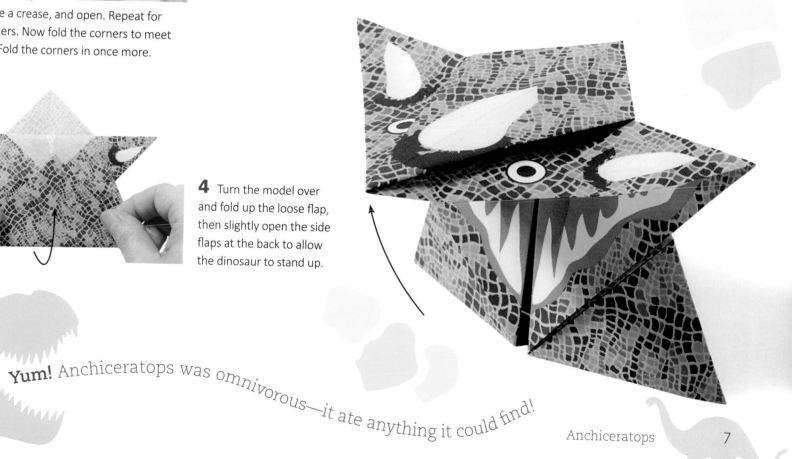

Yum! Anchiceratops was omnivorous—it ate anything it could find!

Dunkleosteus (dun-kel-os-tee-us)

Living about 380 million years ago, this was one of the largest fish ever in existence. It was 33 feet (10 meters) long and powerfully built, with strong armor-plating, but it was also streamlined and shark-like.

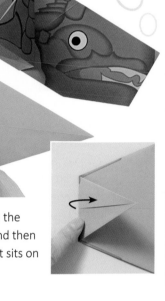

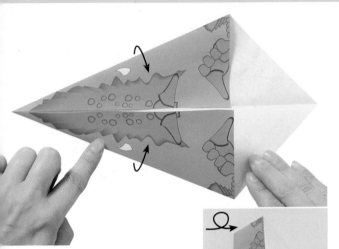

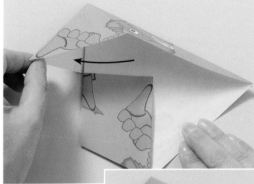

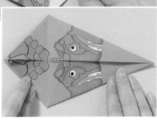

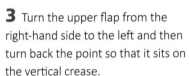

1 Place the sheet of 10in (25cm) square paper with the design face down, then make a crease from corner to corner down the length of the design. Open it out and fold the left-hand edges in so that they meet along the central crease. Turn the object over and fold it in half.

2 Lift the corners of the upper flaps and turn them to the left, refolding the flaps into long points.

3 Turn the upper flap from the right-hand side to the left and then turn back the point so that it sits on the vertical crease.

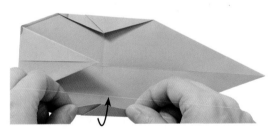

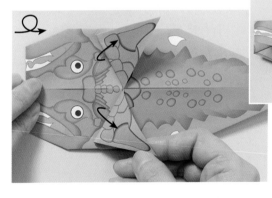

4 Turn the top and bottom points into the middle, making horizontal creases.

5 Turn the model over and fold back the loose flaps at an angle to form the fins. Then fold the model in half along its length.

Snap! Dunkleosteus's jaws were strong enough to bite a modern-day shark in half!

Icaronycteris (ik-a-ro-nik-ter-is)

A very early, extinct member of the bat family, Icaronycteris lived just after the last of the dinosaurs had died out, approximately 50 million years ago. It flew from tree to tree taking its prey, just like modern bats. When you've finished making your model, you can have lots of fun making it fly!

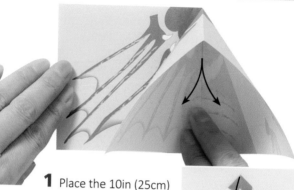

1 Place the 10in (25cm) sheet of paper with the design face down. Fold it in half. Open and repeat in the other direction.
Lift the right-hand side, open out the flap, and refold as a triangle. Turn over and repeat.

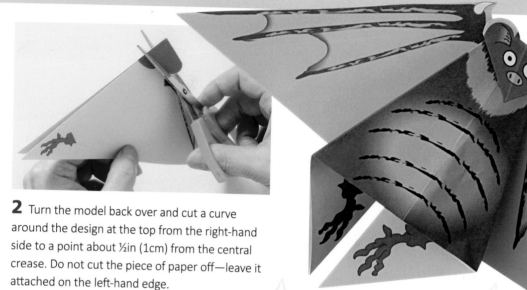

2 Turn the model back over and cut a curve around the design at the top from the right-hand side to a point about ½in (1cm) from the central crease. Do not cut the piece of paper off—leave it attached on the left-hand edge.

3 Fold over the top flap on the left-hand side of the model, so that the edge now runs down the central crease.

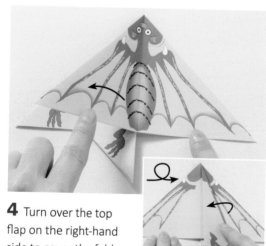

4 Turn over the top flap on the right-hand side to cover the fold just made. Turn the model over and fold the top flap on the right-hand side in half to match that made in step 3.

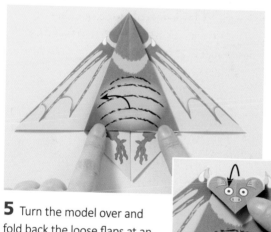

5 Turn the model over and fold back the loose flaps at an angle to form the fins. Then fold the model in half along its length.

Old bat! One of the earliest bats, Icaronycteris lived 50 million years ago!

Ichthyosaurus (ick-thee-o-sore-us)

This small swimming dinosaur's name means "fish lizard." It lived in the seas around modern-day Europe and was the first complete dinosaur fossil to be discovered. It was found in 1811 by a 12-year-old girl called Mary Anning, who loved fossil hunting. She realized the bones looked different to those of fish. Mary went on to become the first female British geologist.

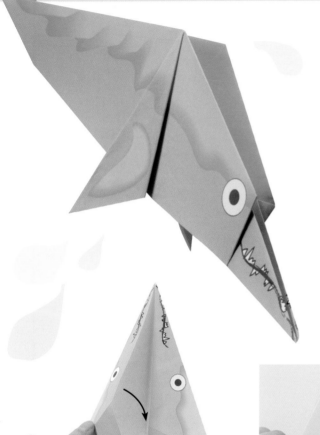

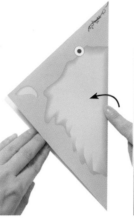 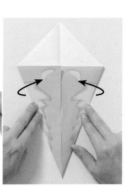

1 Fold the sheet of 10in (25cm) square paper in half from corner to corner through the middle of the design to make a crease. Then open up again and fold in the two side points so that the lower edges of the sheet meet along the central crease.

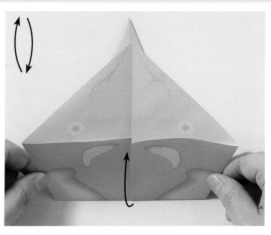

2 Turn the paper over and spin it round, then fold the bottom point up so that it sits on the top point.

3 Lift the top flaps and fold them down, refolding the flaps so that the corners are at the bottom.

4 Fold down the upper flap of the model from the top to make a long diamond shape.

5 Fold back the bottom point so that the tip sits on the horizontal crease, and make a new crease.

6 Fold down the same tip, making a new crease about ½in (1cm) up from the original.

Watch out! A ferocious fish, Ichthyosaurus was at the top of the food chain.

7 Fold the model in half along the main central crease.

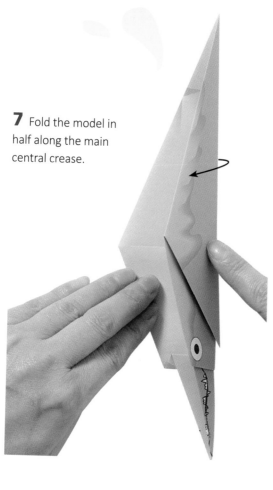

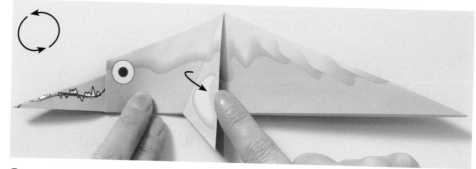

8 Fold the top flaps in half to form the dinosaur's fins, making sure that the diagonal edge now runs vertically.

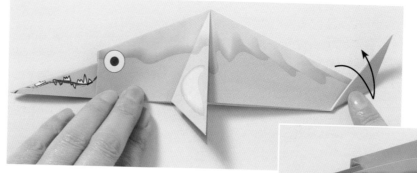

9 Fold over the end of the tail to make a crease, then open out the flap and fold it inside, reversing the direction of the creases so that it stays in place.

Apatosaurus (a-pat-o-sore-us)

Huge and harmless, the Apatosaurus was once more commonly known as the Brontosaurus. Although this dinosaur weighed around 23 tons and was 75 feet (23 meters) long, it spent its days gently eating as much vegetation as possible. Your model won't be as greedy, but it will still be impressive!

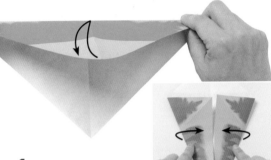

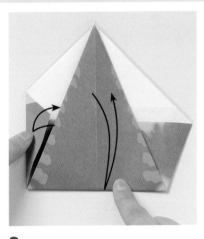

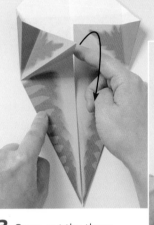

1 First make the rear of the dinosaur. Fold the sheet of 10in (25cm) square paper without the eyes from corner to corner, then open out and fold in the other direction. Open out again and fold the two sides in so that the bottom edges meet along the center line.

2 Fold the bottom point up to the top, then fold in the two side points so that the edges run along the sides of the flap.

3 Open out the three folds made in the previous step, then lift the left-hand flap by the corner and turn it down so that the diagonal crease becomes the horizontal and a new crease is formed underneath. Repeat on the right-hand side.

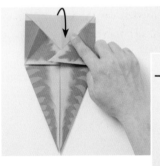

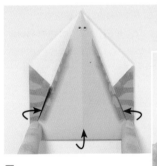

4 Fold down the top tip so that it meets the point in the middle of the model where the two triangles made in step 3 meet. This will cover up any visible white paper. To finish this half of the model, turn the paper over and fold in half along its center line.

5 Take the second piece of paper and repeat steps 1–3 so that it ends up looking as the inset picture above, making sure that the eyes are visible on the narrow point when it is folded up to the top.

6 Fold the paper in half along its length.

Not so clever! Based on brain size, poor old Apatosaurus wasn't very bright.

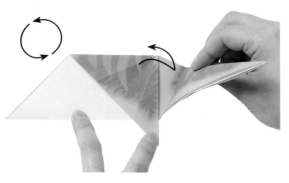

7 Spin the paper through 90° and make a diagonal crease across the neck by turning up the long point so that its bottom edge runs up the side of the triangular flap.

8 Gently open out the paper and push the right-hand end back inside the body, reversing the creases so that it now points up at an angle.

9 Turn over the tip of the nose, making sure that the fold is far enough along that the eyes will become visible in the next step.

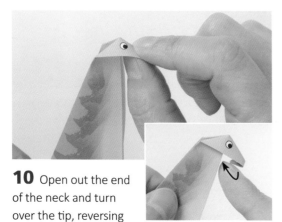

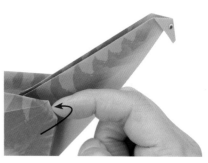

10 Open out the end of the neck and turn over the tip, reversing the crease just made to form the head. Turn the very end inside the flap to form a flat snout.

11 Slide the two sheets of paper together so that the front of the back section slides inside the folds of the diagonal flaps.

12 Turn over the top corners of the front flaps to hold the two sheets together.

Brachiosaurus (brak-he-o-sore-us)

Weighing over 70 tons, this enormous dinosaur was the largest and heaviest land animal that has ever been discovered. It was different from other large, plant-eating sauropods in a few key ways, with longer forelegs than hind legs and a long, more upright neck. Despite its size, Brachiosaurus was a herbivore—it only ate plants!

1 Make the rear of the dinosaur from the 10in (25cm) square sheet of paper without the eyes. Fold it in half from corner to corner both ways, then open out and fold the bottom edges in to meet along the center line.

2 Fold up the bottom to meet the top point to make a crease, then fold in the side points so that the edges run along the edge of the flap.

3 Open out the creases then lift the corner of the left-hand flap, opening out and reversing the folds so that it forms a triangle with a horizontal base. Repeat on the other side.

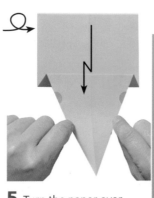

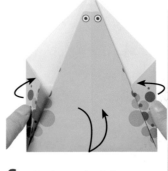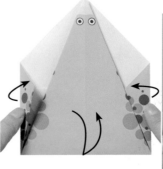

4 Fold down the top point so that the edges run alongside the existing flaps.

5 Turn the paper over and fold the bottom tip back across the horizontal crease before turning back the tip about 1in (2cm) from the fold. Now fold in half lengthways.

6 Take the second sheet of paper and follow steps 1–4, ensuring that the eyes are visible at the end of the narrow point.

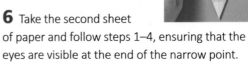

Gigantic! Brachiosaurus was around 100 feet (30 meters) long!

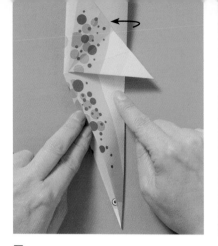

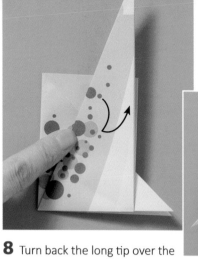

7 Fold the paper in half without including a concertina fold.

8 Turn back the long tip over the horizontal edge then fold the end back at an angle, making a second crease from the point it crosses the horizontal edge.

9 Lift the paper and open it up before pushing the long tip back inside, reversing the creases so that it now sits at an angle.

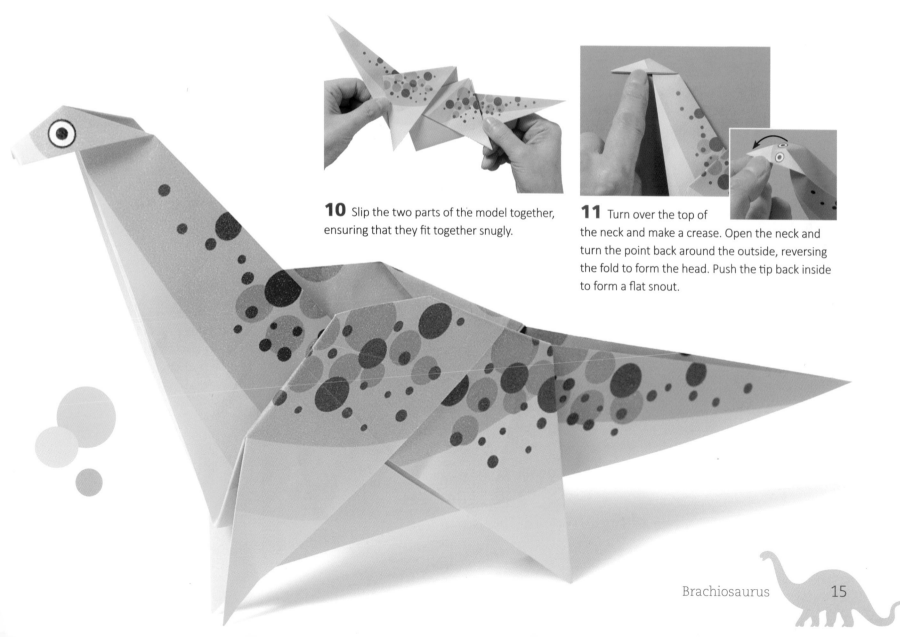

10 Slip the two parts of the model together, ensuring that they fit together snugly.

11 Turn over the top of the neck and make a crease. Open the neck and turn the point back around the outside, reversing the fold to form the head. Push the tip back inside to form a flat snout.

Mosasaurus (moh-suh-sore-us)

The carnivorous Mosasaurus was a marine dinosaur that lived about 65 million years ago. Its huge body, more than 33 feet (10 meters) long, was similar to modern-day crocodiles and it is thought that it swam across the ocean surface, hunting sea turtles and other marine reptiles as well as fish, squid, ammonites, and shellfish.

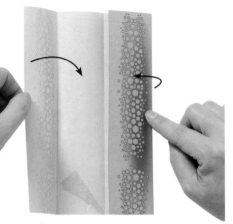

1 Fold the 10in (25cm) square sheet of paper without eyes in half to make a crease. Open out. Fold in the sides to meet along the central crease.

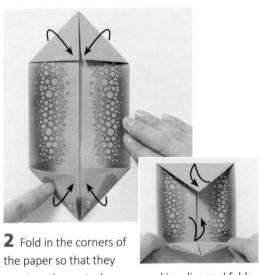

2 Fold in the corners of the paper so that they meet on the central crease, making diagonal folds. Turn up the bottom and top of the model to make crease lines along the edges of these flaps.

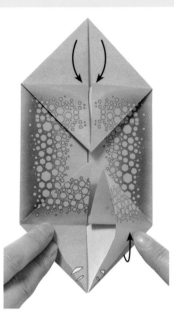

3 Open out the corner flaps and refold them, pushing the corners of the paper sitting on the central crease toward the middle of the model, and reforming the flaps into triangles.

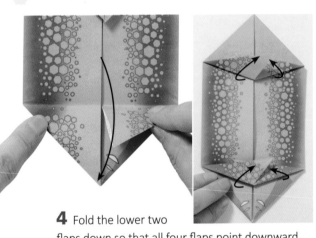

4 Fold the lower two flaps down so that all four flaps point downward, then fold each flap in half so that the diagonal edge runs across the horizontal crease.

5 Turn the model over and fold down the top point across the horizontal crease.

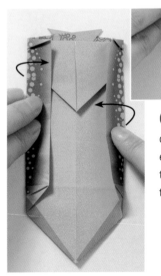

6 Fold in both sides, making new creases about 1in (2cm) from the edge of the paper. Then fold up the bottom diagonal edges along the line where the colors meet.

King of the sea! Mosasaurus was a great predator—very little escaped its jaws!

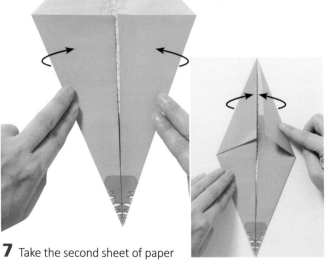
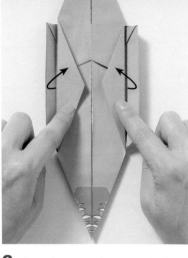

7 Take the second sheet of paper with the eyes and fold it in half from corner to corner down the middle of the design. Then open out and fold in the side points so that the bottom edges meet along the central crease. Repeat with the upper diagonal edges.

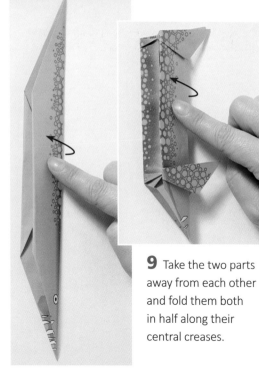

8 Place the second part inside the first and fold over the side points to create vertical edges that match the fold lines inside the first part.

9 Take the two parts away from each other and fold them both in half along their central creases.

10 Fit the parts back together, ensuring that when they are joined up the two diagonal edges create the dinosaur's mouth.

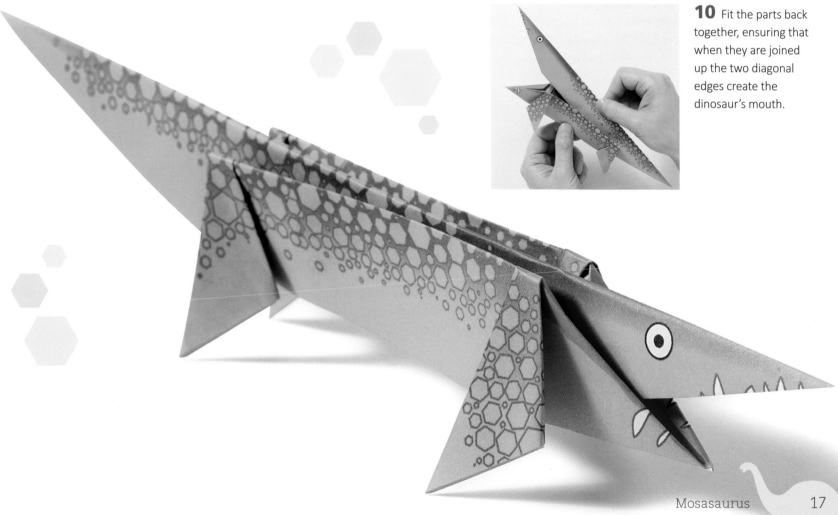

Velociraptor (vell-oss-e-rap-tor)

This fleet-footed dinosaur with massive claws became famous in the movie "Jurassic Park." Lately, though, Velociraptor fossils with traces of feathers have been discovered in China, so it is thought that these "feathered dinosaurs" were, in fact, related to birds. As you make this model, take care to fold all the creases firmly to create the perfect shape.

1 Place the 10in (25cm) square sheet of paper without the eyes with the design face down. Fold it from corner to corner both ways and from side to side both ways. Open out, turn over, and fold the sides into the center.

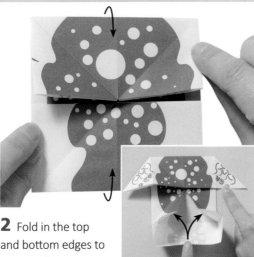

2 Fold in the top and bottom edges to meet in the center, then lift each flap, pushing out the corners and refold to make triangles on each side.

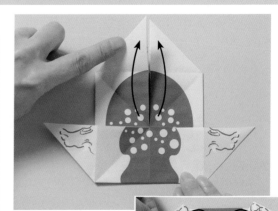

3 Turn the top two flaps up so the points meet at the top of the object, then turn them down at an angle so that the whole shape of each foot is showing.

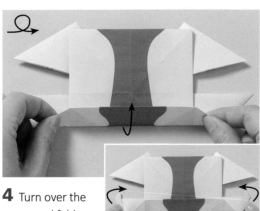

4 Turn over the paper and fold up the bottom edge, so that it runs across the central crease, then turn up the two outer points.

5 Take the second sheet and, design side down, fold it in half then open out and fold from corner to corner through the middle of the design.

6 Open out the paper and fold in the right-hand corner so that it sits on the first crease made in the previous step and the edge of the paper runs up to the top point. Turn the opposite point in so that the edges of the paper meet.

Gotcha! Velociraptor had deadly claws—it would attack its prey in one fell swoop!

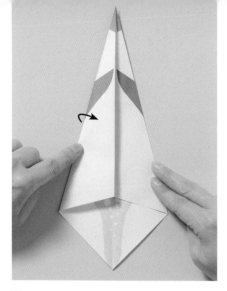

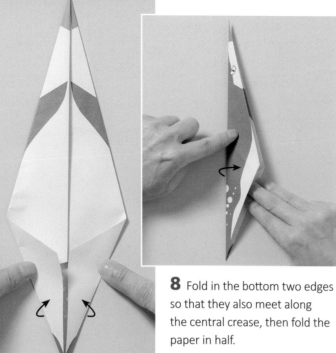

7 Fold over the left-hand side of the paper so that the edge runs down the central crease.

8 Fold in the bottom two edges so that they also meet along the central crease, then fold the paper in half.

9 Place the second sheet on top of the first as shown and close the dinosaur's body around its neck and head.

10 Fold the dinosaur's neck back across the edge of its body and make a firm crease, then release. Make a second fold by turning the head up along the edge of the body.

11 Lift the object up and gently open it out, reversing the folds so that the head sits vertically and inside-out.

12 Fold the neck forward along the top of the dinosaur's body then lift the paper up again and reverse the folds, opening out the head and creating a neck.

13 Turn back the tip of the nose and push it inside the head to form a flat snout, and then prise down the tip to form the tongue.

Velociraptor

Supersaurus (soo-per-sore-us)

At 130 feet (40 meters) long, this dino really was super-sized! Supersaurus is thought to be the biggest dinosaur of the long-necked, plant-eating diplodocus family. As you can imagine, being so huge meant eating all day long. Supersaurus would rake up leaves and vegetation with its feet and swallow it whole to consume the food as quickly as possible!

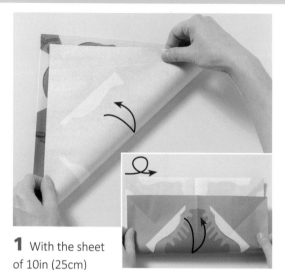

1 With the sheet of 10in (25cm) paper design side up, fold in half both ways from corner to corner, then turn over and fold it in half both ways.

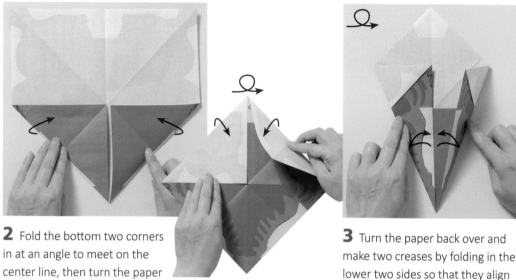

2 Fold the bottom two corners in at an angle to meet on the center line, then turn the paper over and fold forward the top two corners.

3 Turn the paper back over and make two creases by folding in the lower two sides so that they align along the center line. Then open them out.

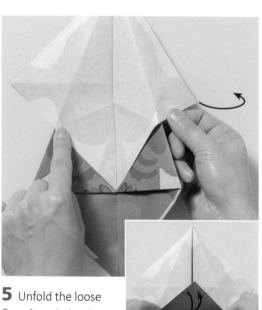

4 Now fold in the upper two edges so that they meet along the center line and press them flat.

5 Unfold the loose flaps from behind the paper to create a diamond shape at the top of the model, then fold up the bottom of the paper to make a horizontal crease.

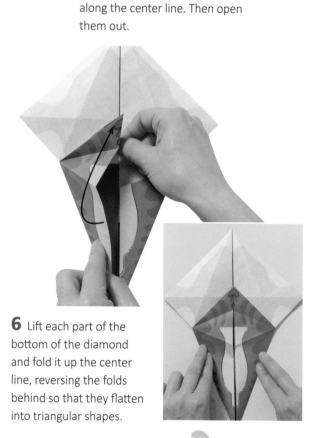

6 Lift each part of the bottom of the diamond and fold it up the center line, reversing the folds behind so that they flatten into triangular shapes.

7 Fold back the upper parts of these triangles to reveal the diamond once again.

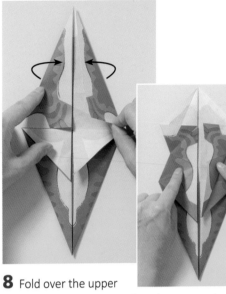

8 Fold over the upper edges of the diamond so that they meet along the center line. Then lift up the bottoms of these edges and turn them up the center line to make triangles pointing down the model.

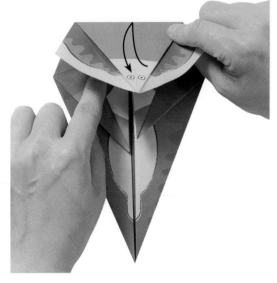

9 Fold the top of the model forward to make a crease.

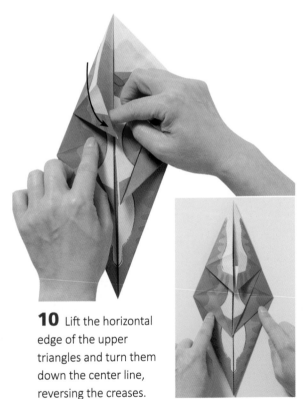

10 Lift the horizontal edge of the upper triangles and turn them down the center line, reversing the creases.

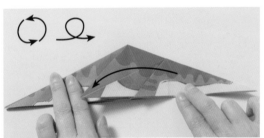

11 Turn the object clockwise 90°, turn it over, and fold it in half, turning the bottom up to the top.

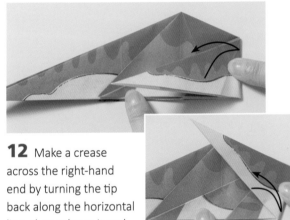

12 Make a crease across the right-hand end by turning the tip back along the horizontal line, then release it and make a second angled crease to its right.

Ouch! Supersaurus used its long tail to whip its enemies.

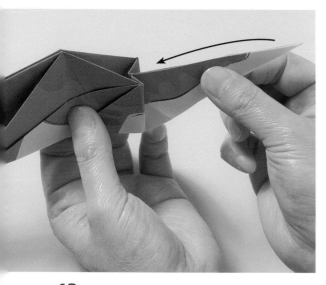

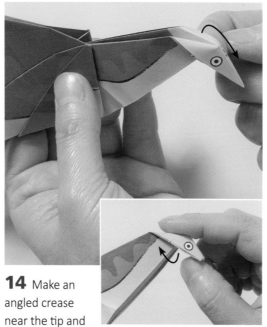

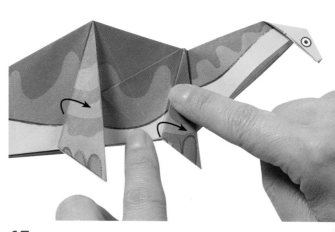

13 Lift up the object and, opening it slightly, push the tip back inside the body of the dinosaur, reversing the creases so that the tip sticks up at an angle.

14 Make an angled crease near the tip and then reverse the fold, turning the end around the outside. Turn up the point inside to create a flat snout.

15 To finish, create the legs by folding the triangles along the dinosaur's body in half, making the left-hand edges run vertically. Turn over the model and repeat on the other side.

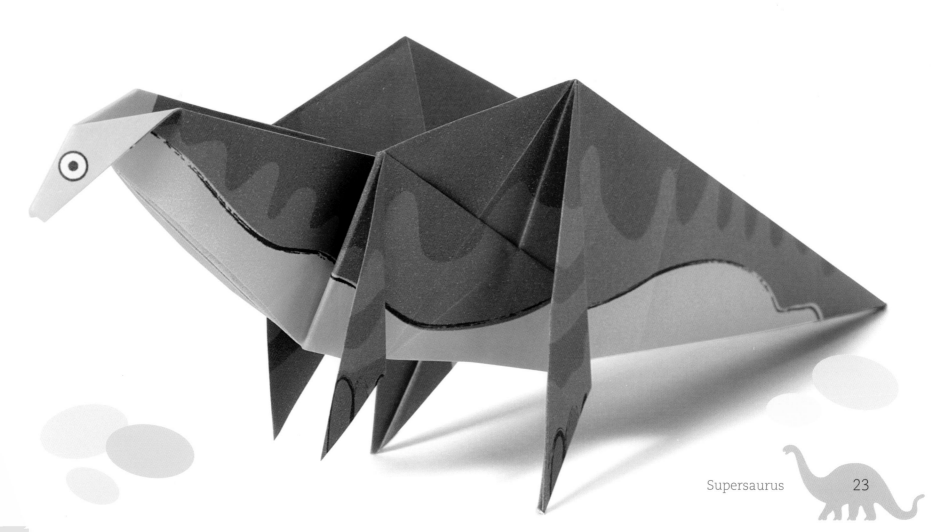

Triceratops (tri-seh-rah-tops)

Triceratops may have been a docile dino, but it was big enough to fight off predators! As you'll see once you've made this dinosaur, the "tri" in its name is due to the fact it has three horns. These were certainly very handy when it came to charging at and fighting off its arch-enemy, the fantastic and ferocious T-Rex (see page 28)!

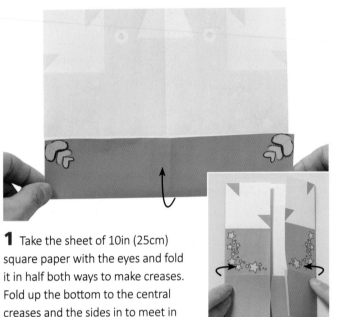

1 Take the sheet of 10in (25cm) square paper with the eyes and fold it in half both ways to make creases. Fold up the bottom to the central creases and the sides in to meet in the middle.

2 Turn down the top two corners so they meet on the center line and then turn the top over to make a crease along the bottom of these new flaps.

3 Lift up each of the triangular flaps and pull out the inside corners from the top, reversing the creases and folding them down the middle of the model.

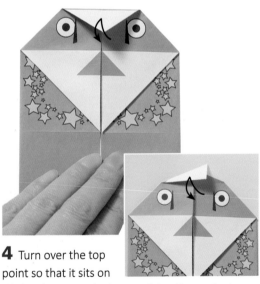

4 Turn over the top point so that it sits on the line between the bases of the diagonal edges, making a crease along the upper edge. Lift the flap and fold both its edges in turn so that they run along the crease line just made.

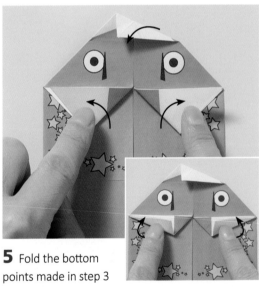

5 Fold the bottom points made in step 3 up and across to the outside of the model so that the vertical edges now run horizontally. Turn up the bottom points on each side so that the outer diagonal edges also run horizontally.

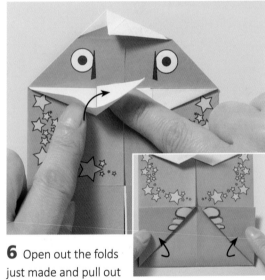

6 Open out the folds just made and pull out the inner flaps, while keeping a finger on the inside. Refold the flap, reversing the inner creases to make a long point across the model, with a new vertical crease inside. Turn up the bottoms of the main flaps so that the vertical edges now run horizontally.

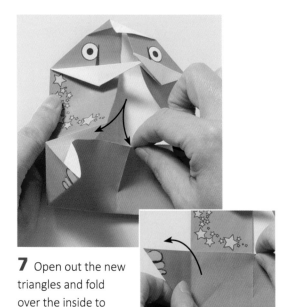

7 Open out the new triangles and fold over the inside to the outside to form triangles.

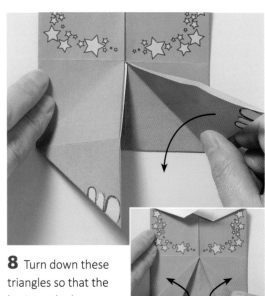

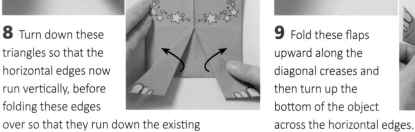

8 Turn down these triangles so that the horizontal edges now run vertically, before folding these edges over so that they run down the existing diagonal creases.

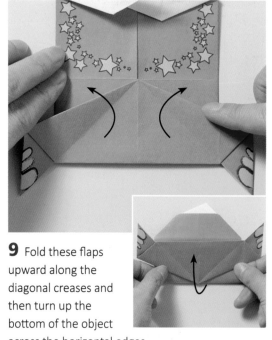

9 Fold these flaps upward along the diagonal creases and then turn up the bottom of the object across the horizontal edges.

10 Take the second sheet of paper and fold it from corner to corner both ways, then fold in both sides so that the lower diagonal edges run up the center of the paper.

11 Open up the paper again and make new creases by folding over the upper edges so that the corners align with the tops of the creases just made. Open out once more and fold in half.

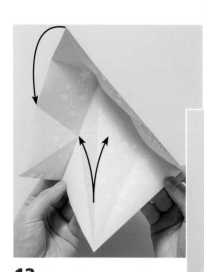

12 Lift up the paper and fold in half again, this time reversing the main length of the central crease so that the edges fold around it, leaving a point at the top of the object.

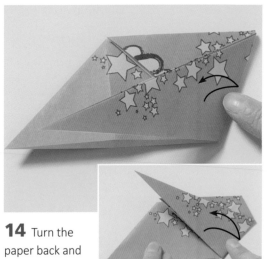

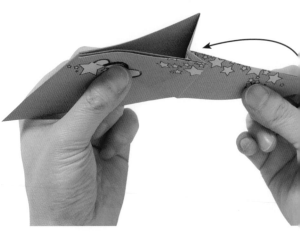

13 Spin the paper through 90° then lift the lower, right-hand corner of the flap and turn it over to the left-hand end of the top edge, making a new diagonal crease from the bottom point. Turn the paper over and repeat on the other side.

14 Turn the paper back and fold over the bottom right-hand point so that it sits on the left-hand point. Open it up again and refold it so that its lower edge lies on top of itself.

15 Now make a concertina fold from these two creases by pushing the long point inside the object to make an angled tail.

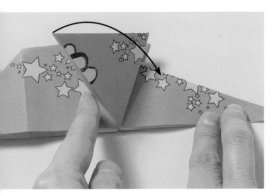

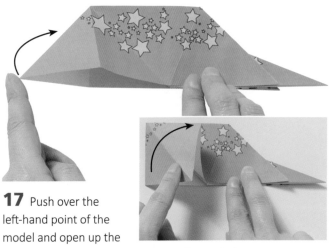

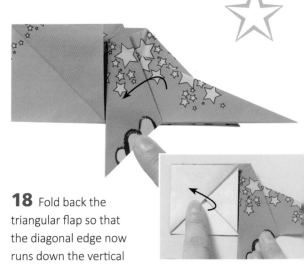

16 Fold forward the triangular flaps on both sides of the model.

17 Push over the left-hand point of the model and open up the piece so that it refolds into a square flap with the point still sitting on the bottom edge of the paper.

18 Fold back the triangular flap so that the diagonal edge now runs down the vertical edge of the square flap. Turn over and repeat, then turn the model back and fold the bottom right corner of the square flap up to the top left corner.

Big head! Triceratops' skull could grow as long as 2 meters (7 feet)!

19 Join the two pieces together. Lift the body piece and turn it over so that you are holding the tail with your left hand. With the nose of the head piece facing the body piece, slide the legs fold over the triangular flap at the back of the body piece until the head piece fits snugly in place.

20 Holding the body piece in your left hand, rotate the head piece toward you until it is at a right angle to the body. The triangular flap of the body piece should now be held in place by the head piece.

21 Press the two sides of the head together to fold the piece in half. As you do this the head will tilt upward until it creates a new diagonal crease in the body piece on which the head sits soundly.

T-Rex (tee-rex)

Tyrannosaurus Rex is by far the most popular and famous of all the dinosaurs. It was strong and ferocious, feared by every other dinosaur. Due to its speed and powerful back legs, its prey would struggle to get away. Its deadly teeth were long and knife-like, causing fatal wounds to its enemies. The largest T-Rex tooth ever found was 12 inches (30 centimeters) long!

1 Fold the sheet of 10in (25cm) sheet of paper with the eyes from corner to corner down the middle of the design, then open out and fold from side to side. Open again and fold the right-hand point across to the second crease line, making a new crease straight up to the top point.

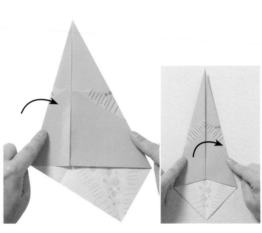

2 Fold over the left-hand side so that the two edges align then fold the left-hand side over again, using the line where the two edges meet as the fold line.

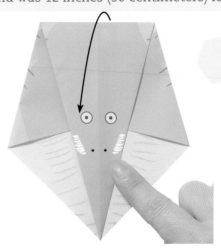

3 Fold the top point down so that it sits on top of the bottom point, making a horizontal fold.

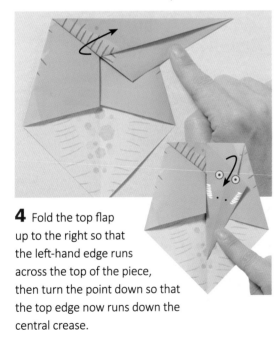

4 Fold the top flap up to the right so that the left-hand edge runs across the top of the piece, then turn the point down so that the top edge now runs down the central crease.

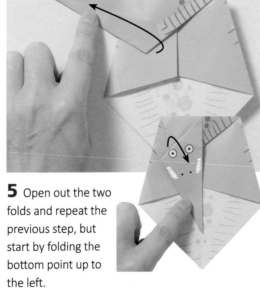

5 Open out the two folds and repeat the previous step, but start by folding the bottom point up to the left.

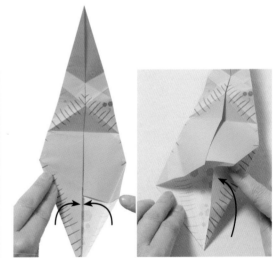

6 Open up the top flap, then fold the short diagonal edges in to meet along the central crease. Lift the right-hand flap, open it up, and reverse the diagonal crease, pushing the fold of paper underneath the top flap.

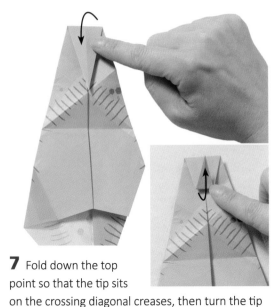

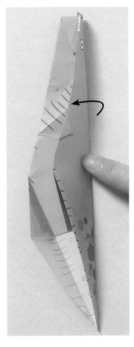

7 Fold down the top point so that the tip sits on the crossing diagonal creases, then turn the tip back up to align with the top of the model.

8 Fold the model in half along its central crease.

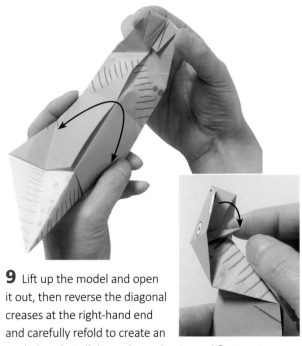

9 Lift up the model and open it out, then reverse the diagonal creases at the right-hand end and carefully refold to create an angled neck. Pull down the end point and flatten at an angle to create the T-Rex's mouth.

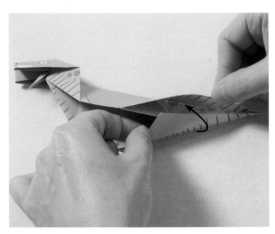

10 Fold the loose paper at the other end inside the opposite flap to hold the body together.

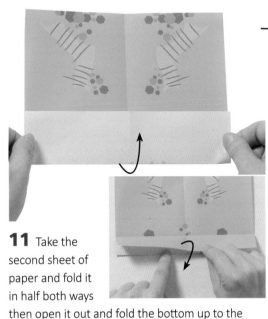

11 Take the second sheet of paper and fold it in half both ways then open it out and fold the bottom up to the central crease. Fold this flap in half by turning it back down to the bottom crease.

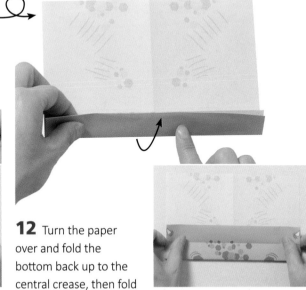

12 Turn the paper over and fold the bottom back up to the central crease, then fold the upper flap at the bottom of the paper over the central crease.

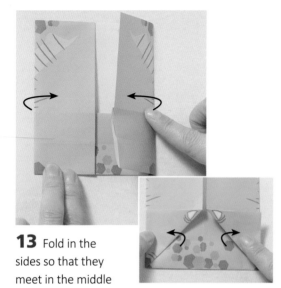

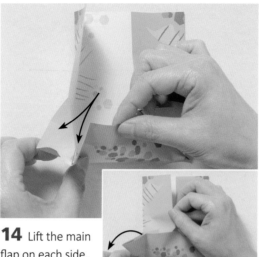

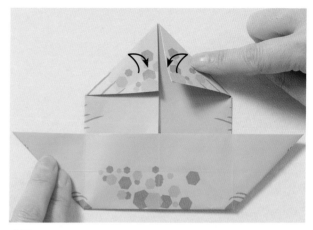

13 Fold in the sides so that they meet in the middle and then turn up the bottom corners of these new flaps, making diagonal creases with the bottom edges now running up the sides of the model.

14 Lift the main flap on each side, opening out the smaller triangular flaps. Then refold the main flaps, reversing the diagonal creases so the smaller flaps now point out over the sides of the model.

15 Fold down the top two corners so that the top edges now align down the center of the model to make two diagonal creases.

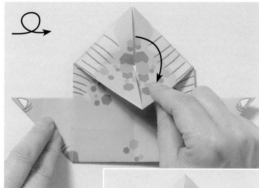

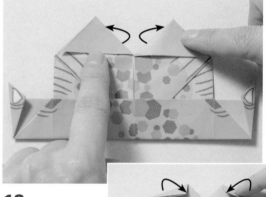

16 Lift the top corners of the model and push them inside, reversing the direction of the creases and refold so that the top of the model is now a single, central point.

17 Turn over the paper and fold down the upper flap from the top of the model. Next turn up the bottom edge so that it runs along the widest horizontal edge. Turn over the outside points using concertina folds.

18 Fold over the two flaps at the top of the model so that the vertical edges run horizontally. Fold over the outside diagonal edges of these new triangles so that they also run horizontally.

Naughty! T-Rex didn't always hunt—it stole meat from other predators.

19 Lift the last flaps and open them out, then refold into the same shape while reversing the direction of the creases so that the flaps are on the outside. Turn these flaps up to the vertical.

20 Fold the opened-out second sheet around the body of the dinosaur and tuck the front corners of the second sheet up inside the body to hold the two pieces of paper together.

T-Rex   31

About the authors

Mari Ono is an expert in origami and all forms of papercrafts. Born in Japan, she has lived in the UK for many years with her artist husband, Takumasa, where they both work to promote Japanese arts and crafts. Her other books include the best-selling *The Simple Art of Origami, Origami for Children, More Origami for Children, How to Make Paper Planes and Other Flying Objects, Wild and Wonderful Origami, Origami for Mindfulness*, and *Origami Farm*, all available from CICO Books.

Hiroaki Takai is an origami master based in Japan. Born in Tokyo in 1957, as a child he fell in love with the models found in Kunihiko Kasahara's *Origami Zoo* and was inspired by them to create his own brilliant collection of dinosaurs and animals. He is the author of many origami books in his native Japan.

Suppliers

Origami paper is available at most good paper stores or online. Try searching online for "origami paper" to find a whole range of stores, selling a wide variety of paper, that will send packages directly to your home.

UK

HOBBYCRAFT
www.hobbycraft.co.uk
TEL: +44 (0)330 026 1400

JP-BOOKS
www.jpbooks.co.uk
TEL: +44 (0)20 7839 4839
info@jpbooks.co.uk

JAPAN CENTRE
www.japancentre.com
TEL: +44 (0)20 3405 1150
enquiry@japancentre.com

THE JAPANESE SHOP
www.thejapaneseshop.co.uk
info@thejapaneseshop.co.uk

USA

A.C. MOORE
www.acmoore.com
Stores nationwide
TEL: 1-888-226-6673

HOBBY LOBBY
www.hobbylobby.com
Stores nationwide

JO-ANN FABRIC AND CRAFT STORE
www.joann.com
Stores nationwide
TEL: 1-888-739-4120

MICHAELS STORES
www.michaels.com
Stores nationwide
TEL: 1-800-642-4235

HAKUBUNDO (HONOLULU, HAWAII)
www.hakubundo.com
TEL: (808) 947-5503
web@hakubundo.com

18 sheets of origami paper

1. Scutosaurus

2. Anchiceratops

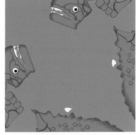

3. Dunkleosteus

4. Icaronycteris

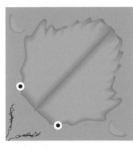

5. Ichthyosaurus

6. Apatosaurus

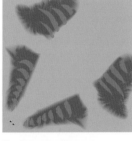

7. Apatosaurus

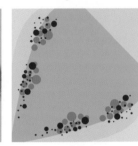

8. Brachiosaurus

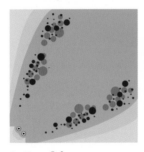

9. Brachiosaurus

10. Mosasaurus

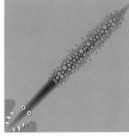

11. Mosasaurus

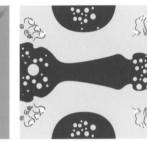

12. Velociraptor

13. Velociraptor

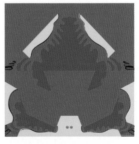

14. Supersaurus

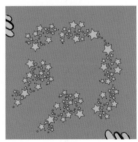

15. Triceratops

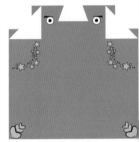

16. Triceratops

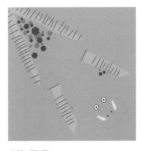

17. T-Rex

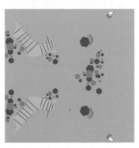

18. T-Rex

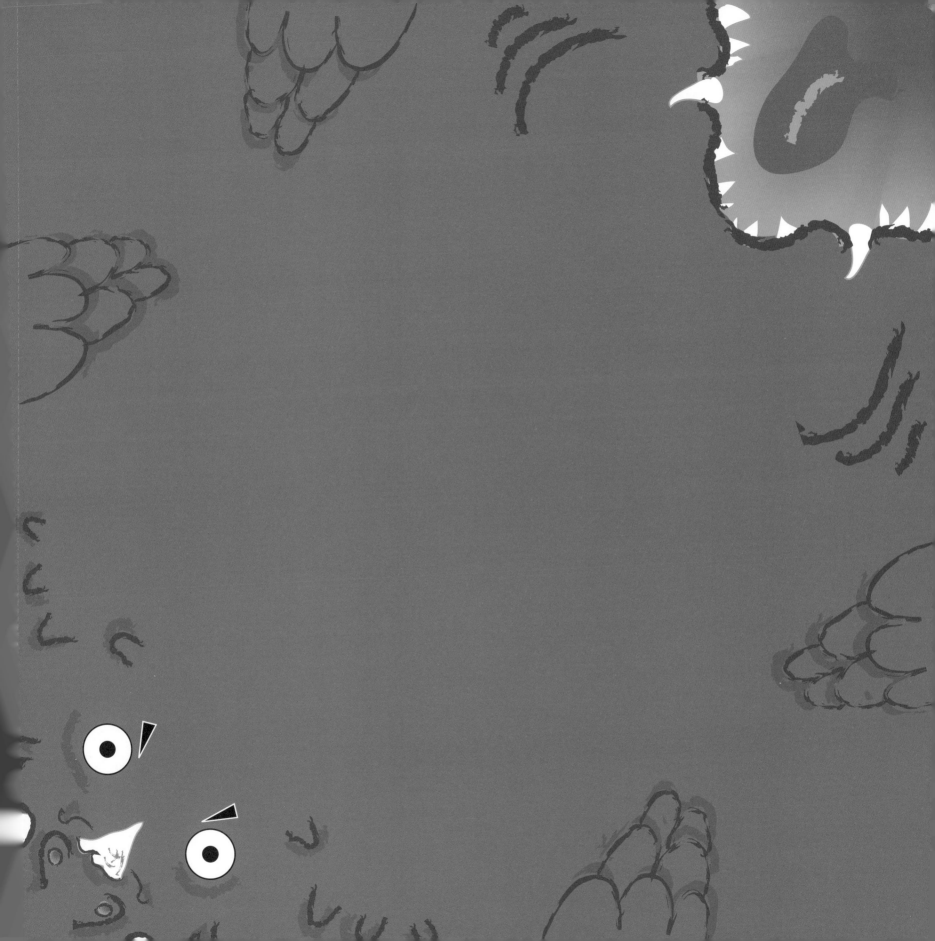

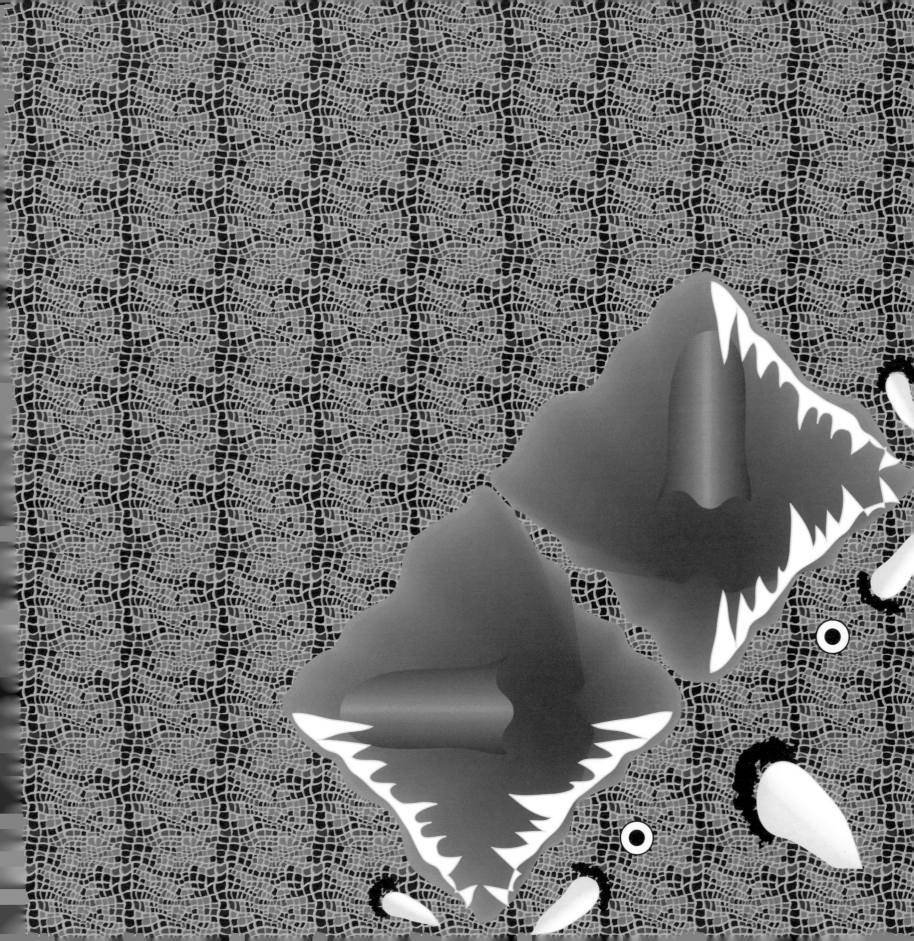

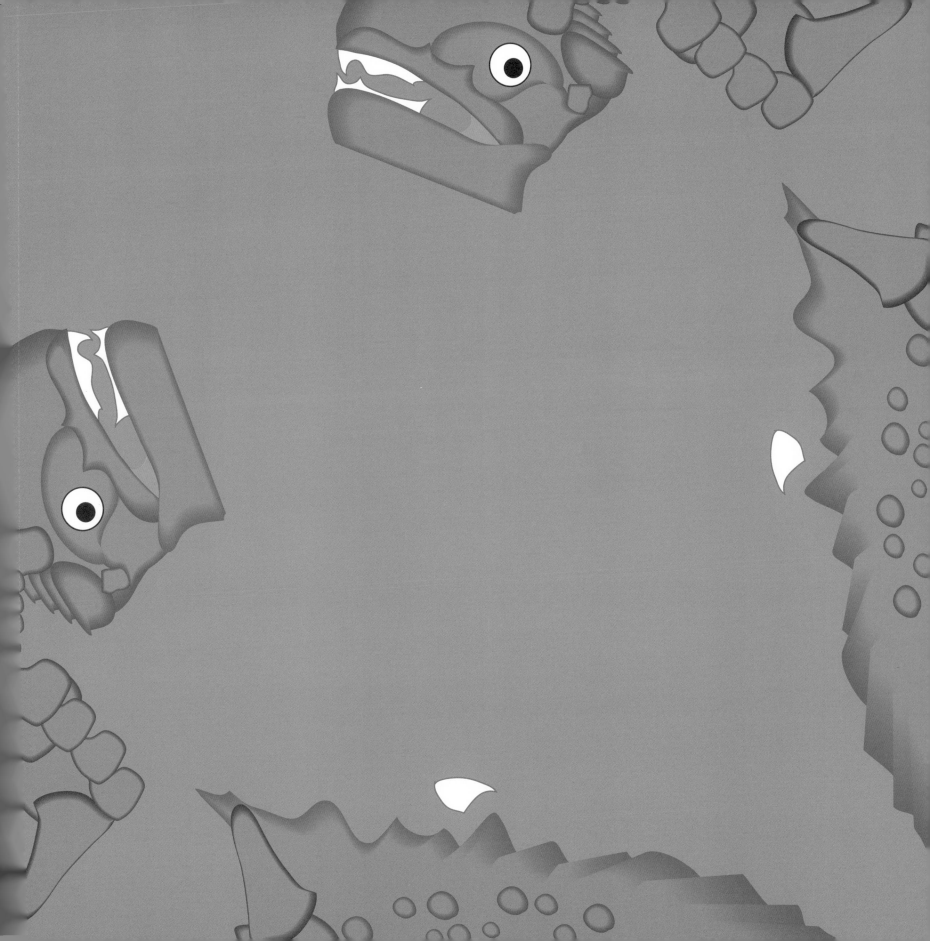

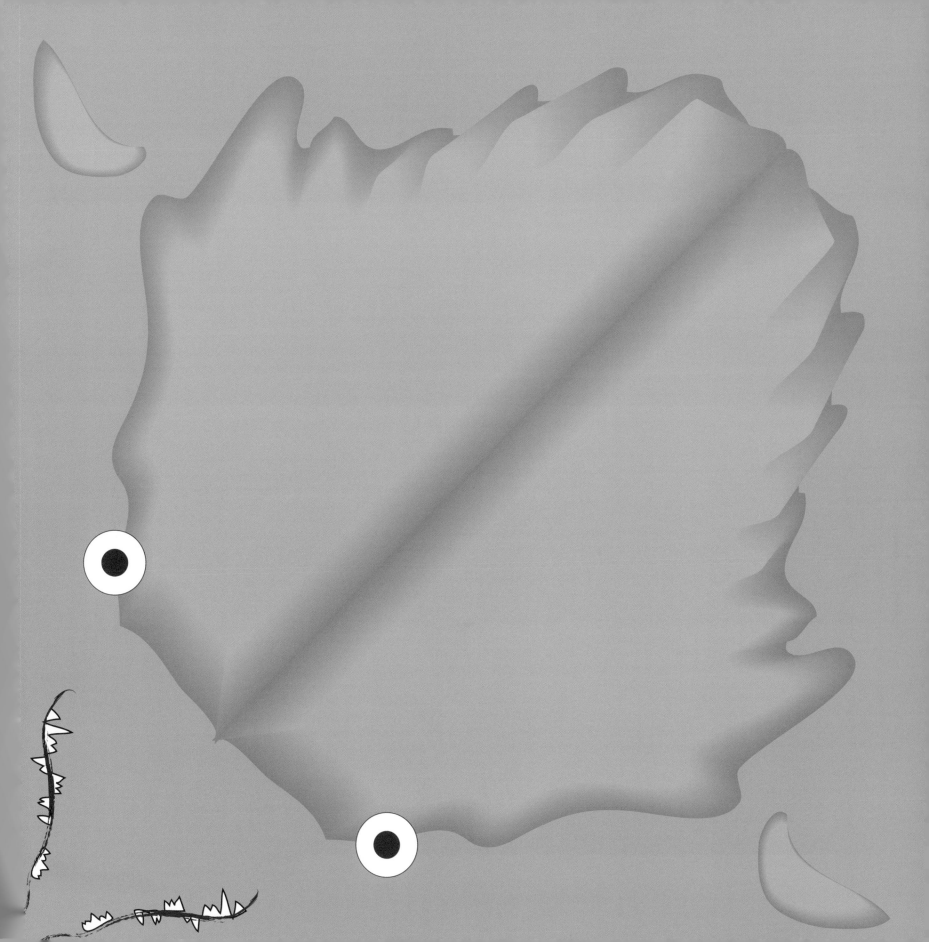

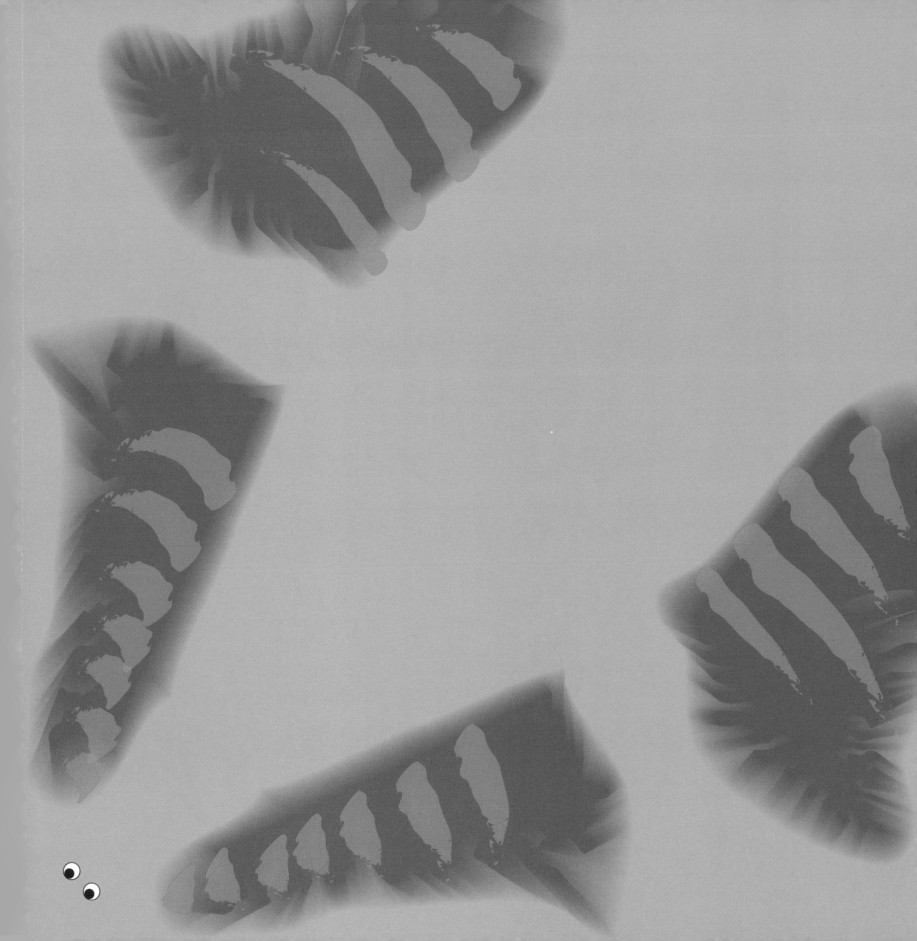

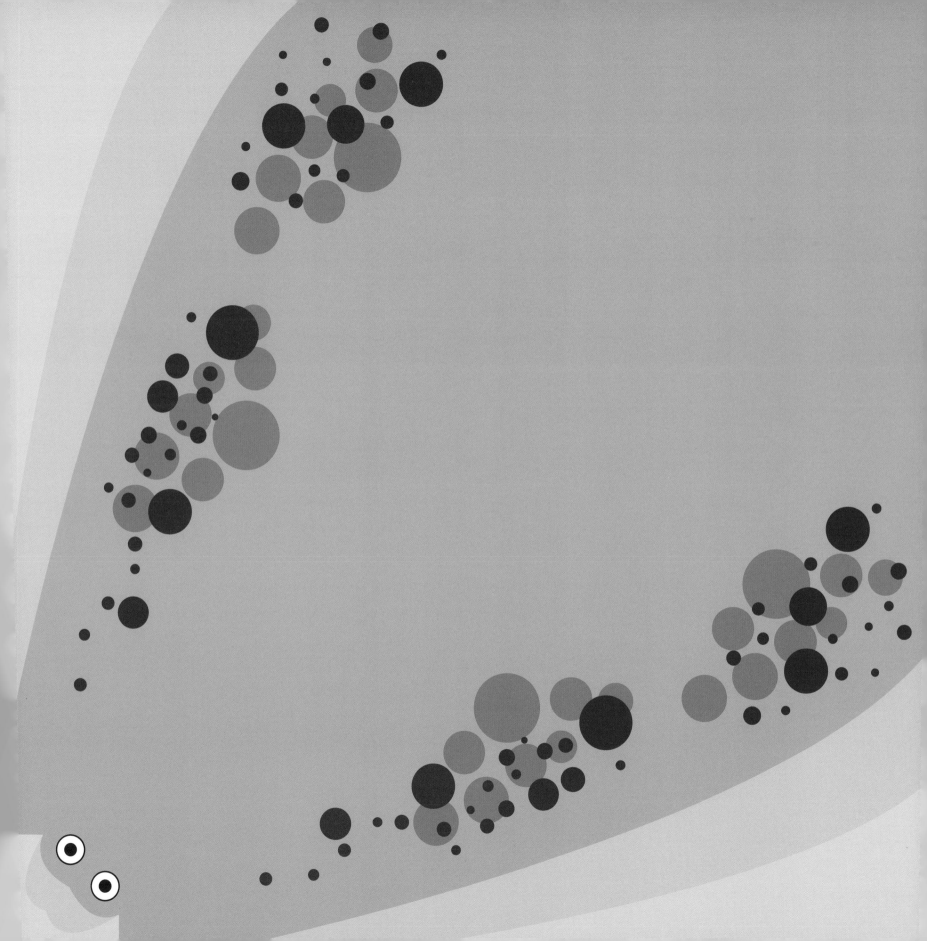

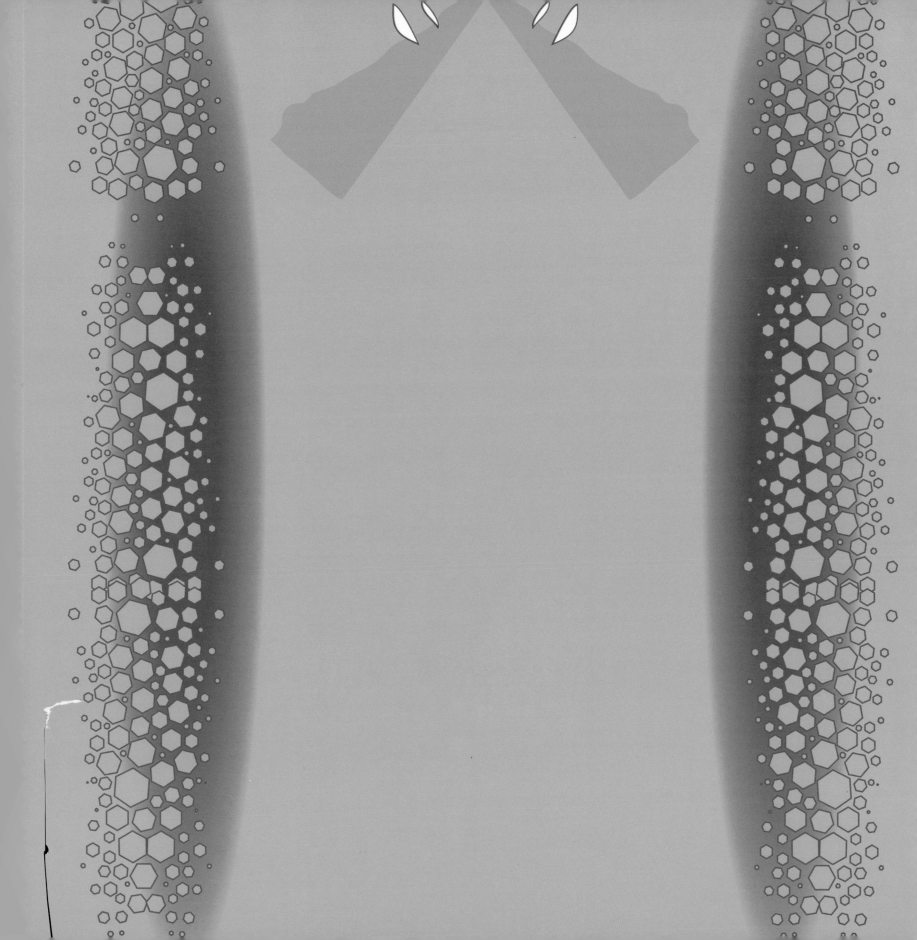

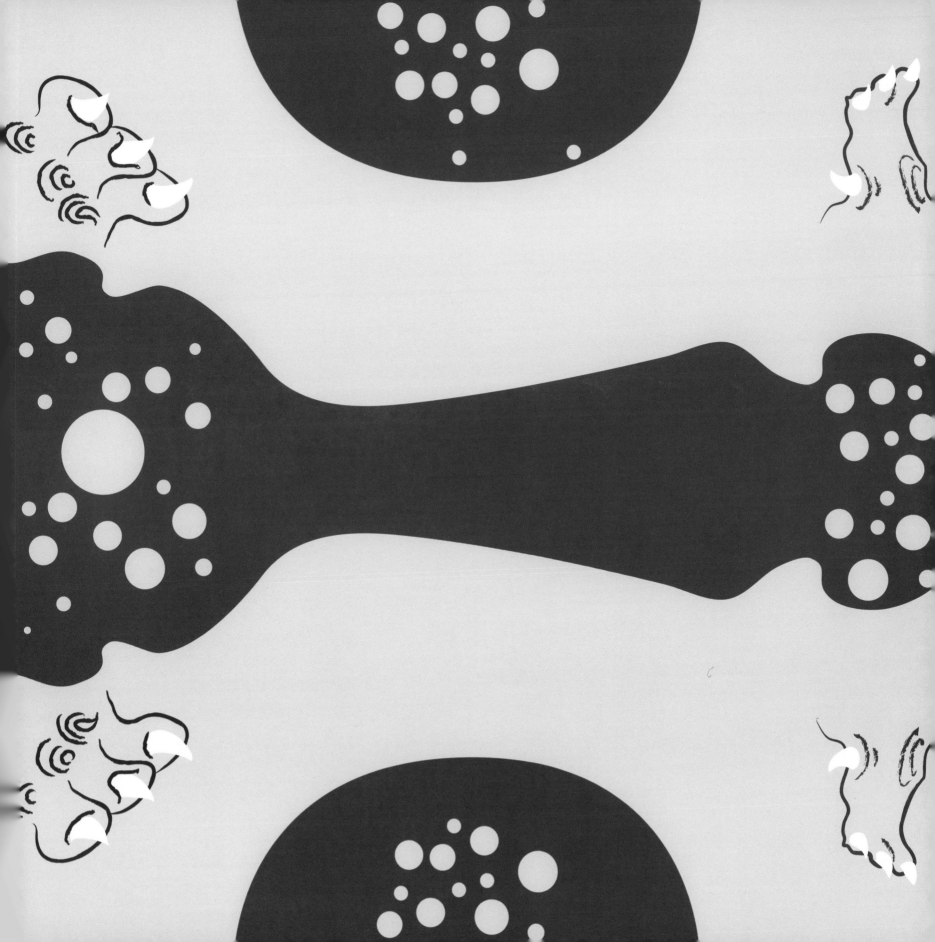

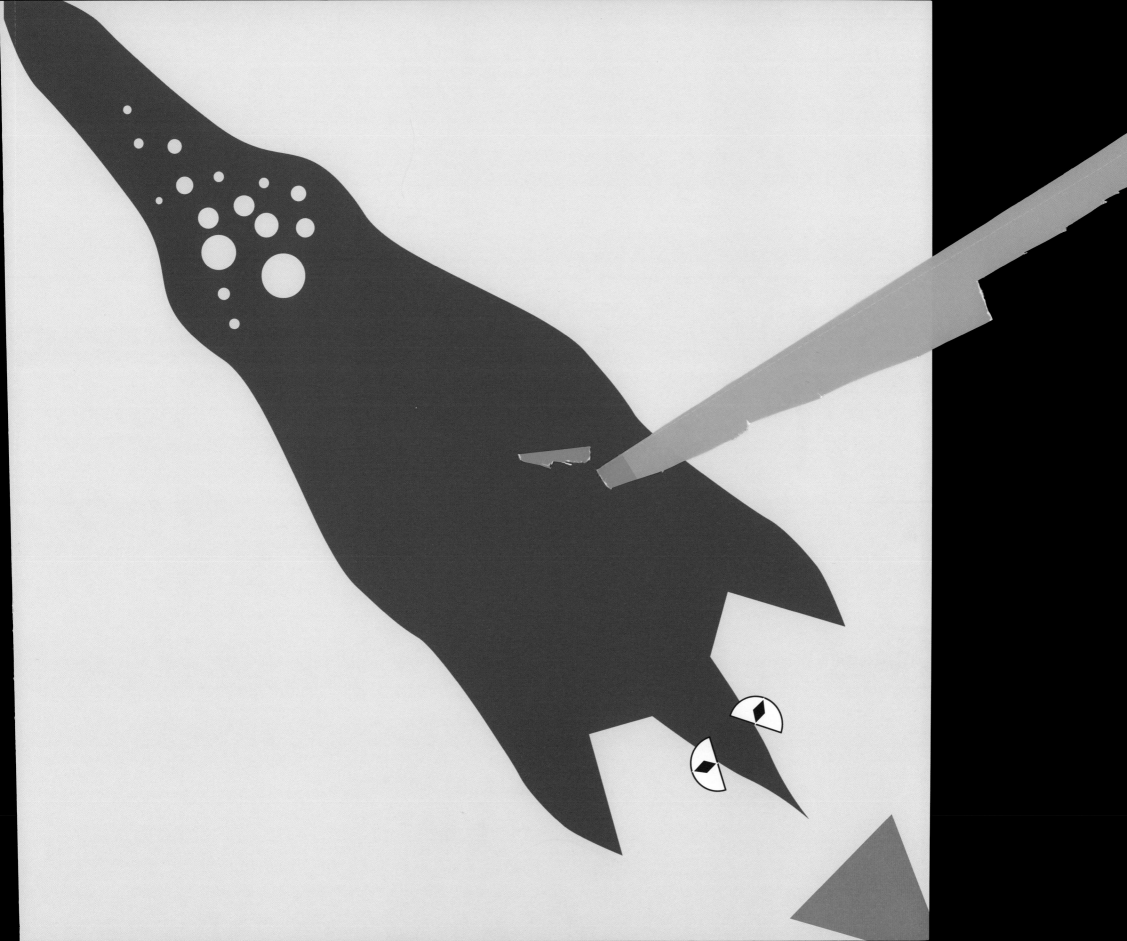

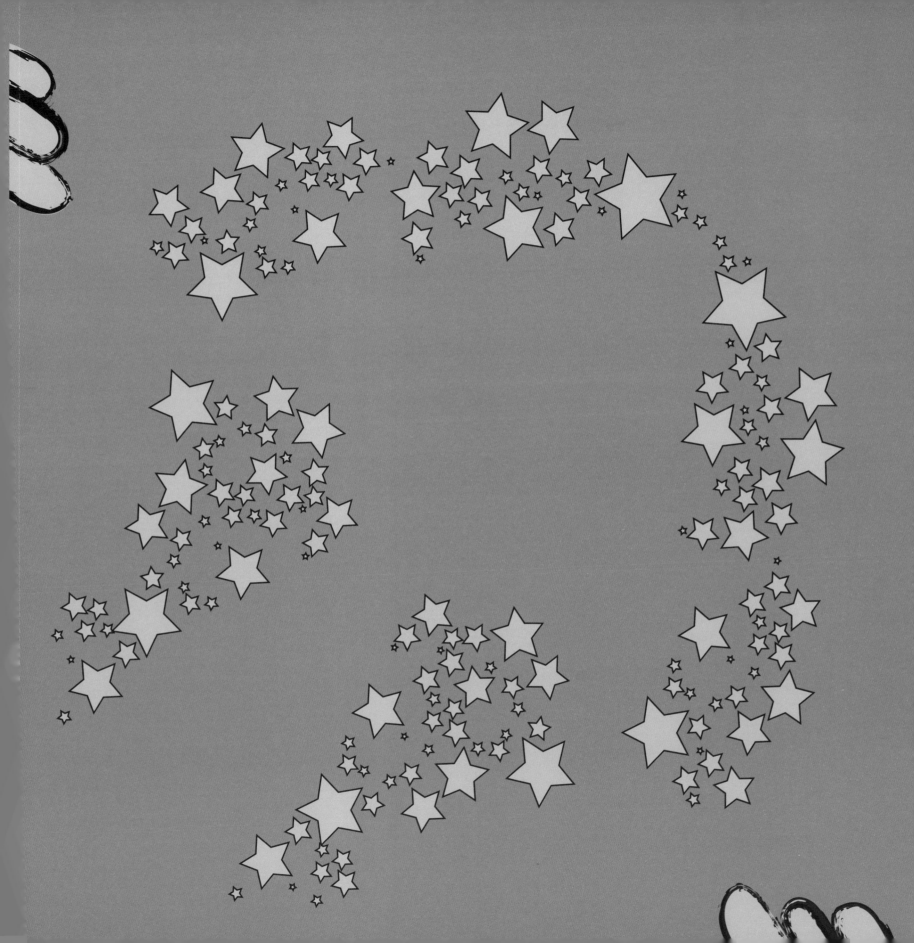

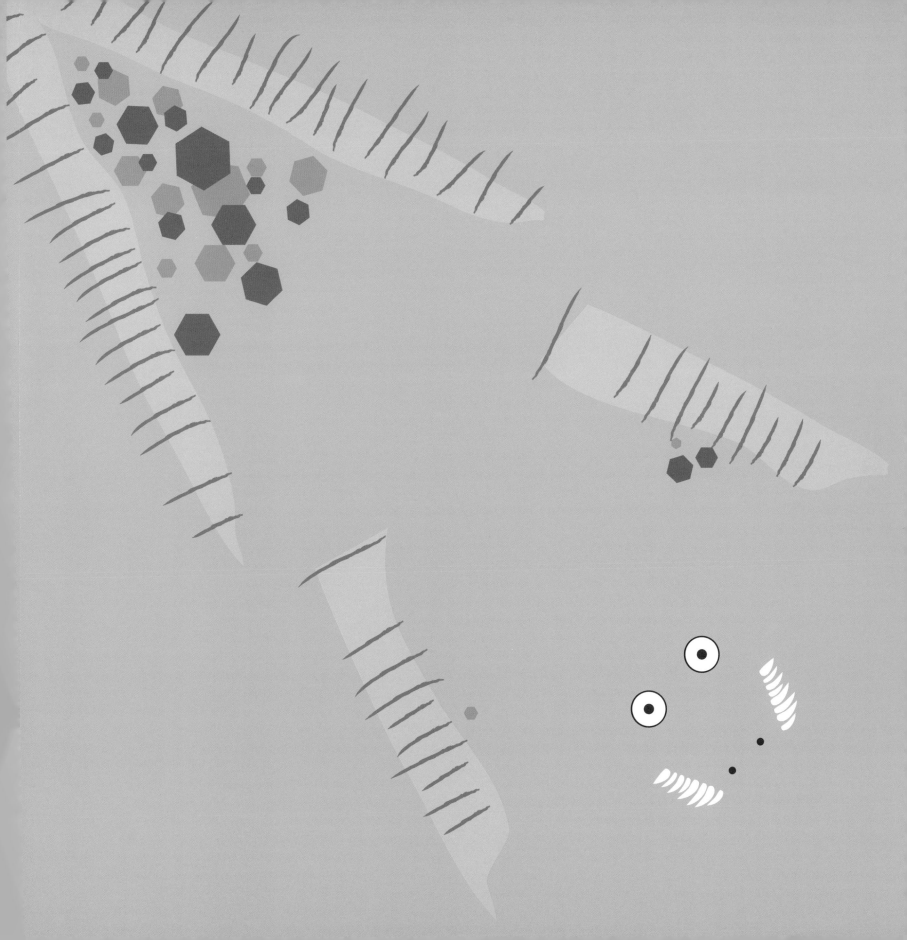